What Living Things Need

Light

Vic Parker

www.raintreepublishers.co.uk
Visit our website to find out more information about **Raintree** books.

To order:
☎ Phone 44 (0) 1865 888112
🖹 Send a fax to 44 (0) 1865 314091
💻 Visit the Raintree Bookshop at **www.raintreepublishers.co.uk** to browse our catalogue and order online.

First published in Great Britain by Raintree,
Halley Court, Jordan Hill, Oxford OX2 8EJ,
part of Harcourt Education.
Raintree is a registered trademark of Harcourt
Education Ltd.

Editorial: Jilly Attwood and Kathy Peltan
Design: Jo Hinton-Malivoire and Bigtop
Picture Research: Ruth Blair and Andrea Sadler
Production: Séverine Ribierre

Originated by Modern Age House Ltd,
Hong Kong
Printed and bound in China by
South China Printing Company

10 digit ISBN 1 406 20036 0 (hardback)
13 digit ISBN 978 1 406 20036 2

11 10 09 08 07 06
10 9 8 7 6 5 4 3 2 1

10 digit ISBN 1 406 20042 5 (paperback)
13 digit ISBN 978 1 406 20042 3

11 10 09
10 9 8 7 6 5 4

British Library Cataloguing in Publication Data
Parker, Victoria
Light. – (What living things need)
571.4'55
A full catalogue record for this book is available
from the British Library.

Acknowledgements
The publishers would like to thank the following
for permission to reproduce photographs: Alamy
pp. **5**, **6**, **7** (Tom Mareschal), **9** (Mike Stone),
back cover (light bulb, Mike Stone); Bubbles
(Loisjoy Thurstun) pp. **11**, **23** (torch); Corbis
p. **4**; FLPA pp. **13** (B. Withers), **16** (Silvestris
Fotoservice), **19** (Colin Marshall), **20** (Roger
Hosking); Getty Images pp. **8** (Stone), **10**, **12**
(Botanica), **14** (Taxi), **23** (shade, Stone), **23**
(vitamin D, Taxi); NHPA pp. **17** (Daniel Heuclin),
18 (Ernie Janes), **22** (Andy Rouse), **23** (shadow,
Andy Rouse), back cover (lizard, Daniel Heuclin);
TopFoto pp. **15** (Bob Daemmrich, The Image
Works), **21** (Gardner).

Cover photograph reproduced with permission of
Alamy.

The publishers would like to thank Michael Scott
for his assistance in the preparation of this book.

Every effort has been made to contact copyright
holders of any material reproduced in this book.
Any omissions will be rectified in subsequent
printings if notice is given to the publishers.

The paper used to print this book comes from
sustainable resources.

Contents

Some words are shown in bold, **like this**. You can find them in the picture glossary on page 23.

What is a living thing?

Living things are things that grow.

People, animals, and plants are living things.

not living

living

Which things in the picture are living and which are not?

What is light?

Light is what stops things from being dark.

Daylight comes from the Sun.

We also get light from light bulbs
and candles.

Is light *just* bright?

Light is hot as well as bright.

This is why it is warm in sunlight, but cool in the **shade**.

Candles and light bulbs get hot
when they are lit.

Be careful not to touch them!

Why do we need light?

We need light to see things clearly.

Take this book and hide in bed.
Can you read the book in the dark?

Find a **torch** and try again.

Can you read the book now?

Is light just for seeing things?

We also need sunlight to keep us warm.

Our bodies need to be warm to stay alive.

Sunlight helps keep our bodies from getting too cold.

Does light keep us healthy?

We need a little bit of sunlight to keep us healthy.

Our bodies get **vitamin D** from sunlight. This helps us to grow.

Too much hot sunlight can make us feel ill.

It can even burn our skin.

Do animals need light to see and keep warm?

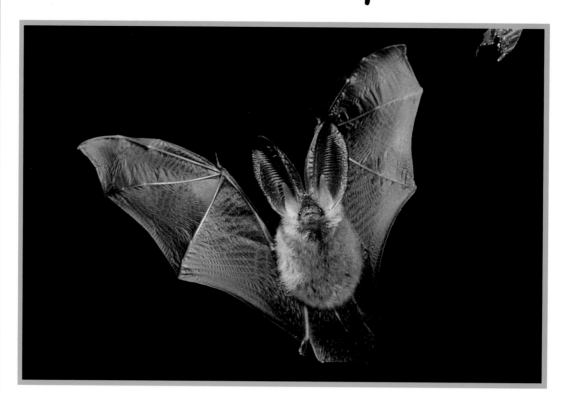

Many animals need light to see. But bats come out when it is dark.

Bats have great hearing. They use it to find their way in the dark.

Many animals need light to
keep warm.

This lizard needs to lie in the sun
to warm itself up.

Do all animals live in sunlight?

Many animals live in sunlight like we do.

But this mole lives under the ground in the dark.

Some animals live in the sea.

The deeper they live in the sea,
the less light they get.

Do plants need light?

All plants need light.

Plants mix light with air and water inside their leaves to make food.

Plants use this food to grow.

Can you guess?

When you stand in sunlight, you make a dark patch. This is called a **shadow**.

Can you guess what is making this shadow? It is a big cat.

Glossary

 **vitamin D** something that our bodies need to grow strong. Our bodies get it from sunlight, and from food such as fish, milk, butter, and eggs.

 **shade** an area out of sunlight, that is dark and cool

 **shadow** the dark shape made when an object blocks out light

 **torch** a type of lamp you can hold in your hand

Index

Note to parents and teachers

Reading non-fiction texts for information is an important part of a child's literacy development. Readers can be encouraged to ask simple questions and then use the text to find the answers. Most chapters in this book begin with a question. Read the questions together. Look at the pictures. Talk about what the answer might be. Then read the text to find out if your predictions were correct. To develop readers' enquiry skills, encourage them to think of other questions they might ask about the topic. Discuss where you could find the answers. Assist children in using the contents page, picture glossary and index to practise research skills and new vocabulary.